BECK

LORD ONLY KNOWS

By Steven Hamer

Created by Pop Culture,

published by OZone Books

a division of Bobcat Books,

distributed by Book Sales Ltd.

Newmarket Road, Bury St. Edmunds,

Suffolk IP33 3YB

Copyright © 1997 OZone Books

Order No: OZ100034

ISBN: 07119 6784 9

Picture credits: All Action, Rex features, Retna

Cover Picture: Rex Features

 POP CULTURE

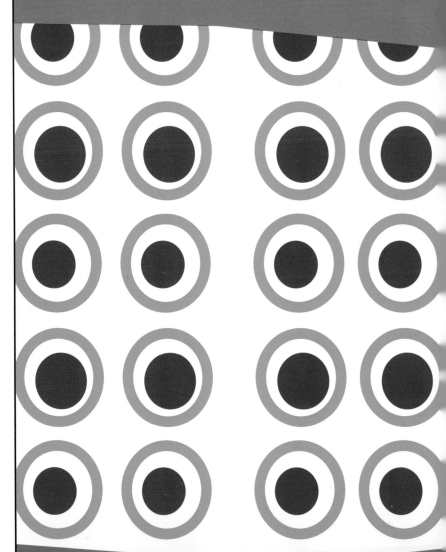

Without whom... Nina Patel, Samina Zahir, Steven Garmson, Pete Hamilton, Jamie Unwin, Emily Millward and Mick Wall

BECK

LORD ONLY KNOWS

By Steven Hamer

CONTENTS

Introduction

When Beck's first Geffen album Mellow Gold was released in Spring 1994, the US monthly music magazine Rolling Stone, described him as 'Woody Guthrie meets Woody Allen'. He's also variously been hailed as 'The King of the Slacker Generation', a 'weird and wacky man-child', 'The coolest living American' and 'the most prolific lyricist of his generation'.

His music defies easy categorisation, due to the very fact that its hybridised eclecticism swerves, shimmies and dodges past any of the labels which are bandied about. While Beck cites just about every musical genre as influencing and infecting his style - even music he considers to be terrible - there's never a sense that he lingers on any one of them more than the next. Neither does he take anything from any of these genres without deconstructing them, exploring them and fitting them back together into his own inimitable style. And, while other artists are happy to wear the influences loud and proud on their sleeves, Beck's more inclined to eat them, digest them and spew 'em out like a bionic human combine harvester.

He could have been the coolest living American, but, quite frankly, he doesn't care for anything 'cool'. And if you're looking for a story about rock'n'roll debauchery: hotel trashing, whiskey-swilling and gang-bang-thank-you-mam groupie-shagging, Beck's most definitely not your man. The nearest Beck gets to a cocaine nose job is through his lyrics. There are no 'Hammer of the Gods' style tales of red snappers, no lurid tabloid headlines, no sensational stories of inter-band or rival-band bust-ups. Beck is definitely a no-scandal zone.

Apart from that, what is so unique about Beck is that he doesn't aspire to be anybody other than himself, whoever that is. He doesn't need to rip off The Beatles or Woody Guthrie or anybody else for that matter, because he's got tunes which can stand up next to any of his heroes, without looking like second-rate imitations.

If there's anyone who has come of the nineties so far, who has attracted a crowd of admirers as long as your arm, ranging from Alan Ginsberg to Tom Petty, from Johnny Cash to Garbage's Shirley Manson - it's Beck. And if you want to find someone contemporary who can unite Oasis's Noel Gallagher and Blur's Damon Albarn in mutual approval, then you need look no further than Beck.

One

THE LUNATIC HAS TAKEN OVER THE ASYLUM...

Now, here's a thing. The first memory most of the British public will have of Beck was his appearance on Top of the Pops way, way back in 1993, performing the accidental hit Loser.

A gawky, gangly 22-year-old in a gaudy, satin shirt and vintage pants wider than your living room curtains, swayed centre-stage, self-concious yet awkwardly composed. He looked like he was barely out of high school, with his sun-kissed, dishevelled limp bob hanging around his anaemic-looking and yet-to-be shaved face. But when he opened his mouth as the lazy slide-guitar started up, and the drum loop backbeat haughtily kicked in, the drawling, grizzling gravel-tones of a 50-year-old, 50-a-day,

THE LUNATIC HAS TAKEN OVER THE ASYLUM...

washed-up blues singer filtered out. He could well have been choking on the splinters he was singing about, and if the conflicting signs which his performance already smacked of weren't confusing enough, the lyrics were even more incomprehensible.

He shared the stage with a backing band who looked like he'd done a dawn raid on the nearest old-folks home, that he'd bundled them into a van, driven them to the studio, put them in front of their instruments, and somehow, through some extraordinary stroke of luck, found that these old geezers were luminary musical geniuses, who had awoken from some antiseptic-induced slumber, and had found the child in themselves again.

Beck was so utterly uncool that he transcended it and became the leader of the cool-less generation, and this three-minute performance was so bizarre that you were left scratching your head, thinking 'what the hell ... ???'

The truth of the matter was more sobering, as Beck remembers in UHF, 'I had the old man from Benny Hill playing drums.   We had to send him home, though. He would have died.' So, at short notice, another 80-year-old swinger was found, probably grabbed off the street outside on his way to collect his pension. On-stage, while these white-haired geriatrics got on down with their sitars, the sandy-haired imp launched himself into what was the most ludicrous attempt at break-dancing ever witnessed on national television . It was absurdity in all its gloriousness, geekiness at its goofiest and, even if we never saw hide nor hair of them again, it was a spectacle that we'd never forget.

Two

ONE·HIT WONDER?
NOT ON YOUR NELLY

Let's just cut the middle bit out, just for a while, and forge full-steam ahead to 24 February 1997, just over four years after Beck's first single was released.

The annual Brit Awards, held at London's Earls Court and hosted by the comedian Ben Elton, couldn't have been further removed from Beck's modest beginnings. One of the glitziest events of the British music calender packed in the stars, with performances by Jamiroquai & Diana Ross, The Bee Gees, 1996's biggest surprise - The Spice Girls, The Artist (formerly known as The Artist Formerly Known as Prince, and formerly as just as plain old Prince) and the Manic Street Preachers.

Immediately after The Fugees' performance (earlier winners of Best International Band), came the nominations for Best International Male Solo Artist, and a motlier crew you couldn't have found. The abysmal Bryan Adams, the bonkers Artist Formerly Known as Prince, Babyface, Robert Miles (winner of Best

New International Newcomer) and Beck.

Beck won.

And somewhat unsurprisingly, he wasn't one of the faces sitting amongst the Kula Shakers, makers, shmoozers and losers (baby). The ceremony cut to a 20 second prerecorded, somewhat understated award presentation.

Looking at least two years older than he did four years ago, Beck, in his trademark cowboy hat and nylon shirt, climbed into a caravan, mineral water and paper grocery bag in his hands, to be greeted by Snoop Doggy Dogg in a hairnet. 'Howdy', he drawled as Snoop half-heartedly handed over the statuette. 'What's this?'he asked, removing his sunglasses to reveal yet another pair of specs. 'It's your Brit Award, you know what's happenin' ' - Snoop drawled back. 'Oh wow, oh cool, alrighty. OK.'

Underawed? Well, he tried, but awards aren't what Beck's about when they're voted for by the music biz insiders.

Three

THE ONLY THING I HAVE TO DECLARE IS MY GENES.

Life for Beck has never been grounded or conventional. Little is known about Beck's father, David Campbell. Soon after Beck was born, he flew the nest, setting up home with another woman and starting another family. Campbell continues as a blue-grass musician to this day, and was responsible for composing string sections for many of the Asylum artists including Linda Ronstadt in the '80s, and, amongst other things, was also one of the arrangers for Aerosmith's Nine Lives Album. However, it would be fair to say that his father's influence on Beck has been minimal, and that they've had very little contact since he was born. Beck has even taking the step of renouncing the Campbell name in favour of his maternal name, Hansen.

'I slept under the kitchen

Bibbe Hansen, Beck's mother, was only 18-years-old when she gave birth to her first child. Beck David Campbell was born at home on the morning of 8 July 1971 in Los Angeles. Before motherhood, Bibbe had spent time hanging out in New York. Here, she was the youngest scenester of Andy Warhol's Factory . At only 13-years-old, she was hanging out with the bohemian art and music scene which attracted freaks, geeks and beautiful people - spending her time with the likes of the Velvet Underground, Nico and Edie Sedgwick. She even appeared with Sedgwick in one of Warhol's films Prison ,which was never released. ('It was not the major fact of my life that my mother used to hang out with Andy Warhol', Beck has since commented in The Guardian.) Once she'd had her fill of New York, Bibbe headed back west to Los Angeles, where she has stayed ever since.

Times were hard for Bibbe after Beck was born, and without having Beck's father around to help her out, Beck found himself spending a large part of his early years in Kansas with his paternal grandmother and father, a Presbyterian minister. In total contrast, Beck would periodically go back to stay with his mother in a poor Latino suburb of East Los Angeles. It wasn't a rare occurrence for a nine-year-old Beck to come down in the morning to find the living room couch occupied by some down-on-his-luck punk that Bibbe had taken pity on. This included, Bibbe claims, the Screamers, the Controllers and perhaps most famously, LA's most infamous punker, (the late) Darby Crash of The Germs.

When he was 12, Beck moved to South Vermont Avenue in Los Angeles to live full-time with his mother and Mexican step-father, and eventually became the big brother to four siblings, including his half-brother, Channing. 'We lived in a one-bedroomed apartment and there were five of us, so I never had any space at all', he recalled in The Face. 'I slept under the kitchen table in a sleeping-bag.'

Compared to the relative normality of his upbringing with his grandparents in Kansas, Bibbe opted for a more unorthodox 'hands-off' approach to child-rearing, letting her kids do their own thing, while she did hers. This, however, didn't pose a problem for Beck: 'I don't think anybody had a conventional upbringing. Our parents were part of the generation where music was exploding and everybody was experimenting with drugs', he told Papermag when asked about his upbringing. 'The whole "Leave It to the Beaver" idea of the family never existed for us. It's just something on TV.'

His neighbourhood was pretty rough, a cultural mix and mismatch, whose only common link was their bad luck and lack of opportunity. He spent much of his childhood finding low-budget things to keep himself amused. And, as he explained to Cliff Jones of The Face, he was a bit like a square peg in a round hole. 'I was the only white guy in the neighbourhood, so I felt completely alienated from suburban white culture, even intimidated by it. I couldn't relate to kids my own age and colour, because I didn't live the way they did. But at the same time, I couldn't hang out with the Salvadorian gangs on the street, 'cause to them I was the "Whetto", the weird white kid.'

Surprisingly, Beck seems to bear none of the obvious psychological scars you'd expect from being something of

table in a sleeping-bag.'

a cultural outcast. The only discernible effect was that he soaked up the diversity of cultures like a thirsty sponge. Everything he heard stuck in his memory, from the Brazilian music blasting from car stereos, to the kids breakdancing on the streets with their ghettoblasters. The fact that Beck didn't have the material things that your average white American kids had didn't bother him, because neither did anyone else in his neighbourhood. However, what he did have, was a core of people who actively encouraged his autonomy and self-development, though not through neglect, and it was more a case of leaving him to his own devices, and giving him the space to discover things for himself.

One of his major influences was his mother's father - Al Hansen. Born in 1927, Al married Audrey, a poet, actress and model, but in 1968, three years before Beck was born, she died. In Al Hansen, you couldn't have found anyone who was more different to Beck's paternal grandfather if you'd tried. Whilst the latter was relatively conservative and conventional, Al was pretty much out there - never surrendering to the rigours of old age.

Al was a key member of Fluxus, the celebrated, iconoclastic art-house movement which was founded in the late 50s, and pioneered by John Cage of the New School for Social Research. Fluxus was described by The Guardian as 'An exploration of the 1960s art movement, whose eccentric activities included the production of curious stage shows, "happenings" and Dadaist films and artwork.' In other words, it was about as avant-garde as you can get', and challenged conventional views of art.'There is a man in New York and his name is George Brecht', recalled George Macuinas on Radio 3. 'And he does a work of art which is limited - he blinks, and he says, "That's a work of art", he shakes a hand and says, "That's a work of art." '

Well, we'll come back to you on that one George, don't call us! The most famous Fluxus member was Yoko Ono, who took part in unusual performances where her fellow artists would cut all her clothes off with kitchen utensils. Although Fluxus was a middle-class movement and Beck's influences and background is working-class, the theory behind the movement's approach favoured deconstruction with an 'anything goes' outlook, and this was to flavour Beck's approach to his music.

Although Beck and Al didn't get really close, his approach to life and his art had a real effect on Beck. As he told Papermag, 'I didn't have a lot of contact with my grandfather, but seeing how he worked gave me confidence ... In seeing that, I never felt that I had to have schooling in order to create. He was this presence; he got people excited about that scene.' It was indeed Al who introduced Bibbe to Warhol and punk, and who got Beck and Channing involved in his overtly avant-garde art projects.

'I remember him wanting to buy my old plastic rocking horse when I was a kid', he told UHF. 'It was sitting in the garage all covered in dust. He gave me five dollars for it, and when I came home from school later that day, the thing was decapitated and covered in cigarette butts and spray-painted silver. I was horrified, but also electrified at the possibility of taking something that was useless and turning it into a beautiful monstrosity.'

Whereas Channing was to follow closely in his grandfather's footsteps, studying at the San Francisco Art Institute, and becoming a third generation Fluxus artist, Beck was to take a different route, and though being part of a scene, he would find himself bending the rules and challenging conventionalist ideals.

Four
MUSICAL BEGINNINGS

When he was about 14, Beck's already smouldering passion for music was set alight. Not through anything so contemporary as his mother's passion for punk, but by the old Delta Blues and folk artists like Woody Guthrie, Leadbelly, Mississippi John Hurt, Blind Willie Johnson and Charley Patton. Up until then, he'd been left unmoved by most of the music which he had been exposed to, and as he told The Face, he was 'looking for something more honest in music.' For Beck, Delta Blues was exactly that. Because he never had any space to be alone at home, he'd spend long hours sifting through reams and reams of vinyl in the public library like a laid-back man possessed.

'I started poking around the book and the record sections, and found an old Mississippi John Hurt record, and he was this wrinkled-up guy on the cover, and he looked so intense I thought "whoa, this is incredible, I must hear this" ', he told Cliff Jones of The Face. 'This was 1985, the height of the artificial synth pop, no-personality, drum-machine, zero-charisma music period - music influenced by greed and materialism. When I found the blues, I was like this is my music, this is what I am.'

It was these old musical veterans who first prompted Beck to pick up a battered, redundant old acoustic guitar which he had found left lying around the apartment. Soon enough, he started to teach himself to pluck along to the small

'I didn't go to high school 'cos I would have gotten killed'

collection of blues and folk 78rpm records he had started to slowly build up.

Nobody in Beck's family batted an eyelid when, aged 16, he made the decision to quit junior high three years before he would have graduated. He gives the various reasons for his early departure : 'I didn't go to high school 'cos I would have gotten killed' (Select), 'I didn't have any friends, and it felt like kind of a waste to me' (Spin), and 'I don't have any good excuses for that, except that it was very tedious and nauseating. I didn't go to a good school' (Papermag).

Whatever the reason, he had all the time in the world to strum along to his new-found heroes. His first public performance was to be in a park near his home. It was here that the geeky, skinny kid would regularly make the pilgrimage to busk away, while the Hispanic footballers practised their football tricks. No one bothered to stop and listen. At best, he'd get blank-faced stares, at worst, passers-by would shout abuse at him. 'It was really pathetic', he confessed in Spin. Yet undeterred, Beck continued working out riffs and licks, and continued with his trips to the park, despite the continued frosty reception.

It was around this time that he took up a well-documented stream of menial dead end jobs, in the Hollywood and Silverlake areas of LA. On his way to work, he'd busk away on the trams, where he'd attract the same response from his fellow commuters as from the people in the park. The jobs he managed to get were all light manual labour, including blowing leaves off the gardens of the over-privileged occupants of Hollywood, painting gaudy signs for lingerie and thrift stores (many of which still remain) and working long hours in a clothes factory. As mundane as these jobs were, they had enough effect on Beck to spin the lyrics of many of his early songs.

However, all his free time was spent perfecting his music. Inventively, he started creating his first demos with the only resources he had to hand - a couple of old cassette recorders. He'd layer track over track, until he was left with a fuzzed-up and distorted confusion. He also graduated from busking in the park, to begging and hassling people to let him play in between sets at LA bars like Raj's and Al's Bar. Due to his age, he joined in with the poetry and spoken-word set because there were no age restrictions, and he was to become one- third of a poetry ensemble, which called themselves 'Youthless'.

His diversifying musical tastes included getting into the likes of Jon Spencer's Pussy Galore (buying one of their records because, as a kid, he was a massive James Bond fan), Sonic Youth and LA's biggest export - hip-hop. The latter motivating him to teach himself break-dancing.

Music as a career though, had never really occurred to him. Due to the fact that he'd left high school with no qualifications, and because his family had little money behind them to help him out, he logically saw his path as necessarily and unavoidably leading to a life of menial jobs. This was the main reason behind his decision to quit the proverbial job blowing leaves, cited in his song Beercan, and get himself out of LA. Though this was not with any flighty ideas about finding his fame and fortune, but instead to have a bit of fun, and see a bit of life, before he was forced to settle into the life everyone else in his neighbourhood had to accept.

Five

N.Y.

It was in 1989 when he was just 18, that he decided to quit LA for a while. There was a special offer for a $30 dollar ticket to anywhere in the States. So he set off one morning on a Greyhound bus heading towards the East Coast, with his bargain ticket in his pocket, his girlfriend on one arm and his old guitar in his free hand. Four sweaty, and often treacherous, days later, they found themselves standing in New York's grey and depressing Port Authority Bus Terminal, with no firm plans except to find somewhere to put their heads down for the night. Soon afterwards, his girlfriend was to desert him, but thankfully, his guitar was more faithful.

He soon gravitated downtown to the Lower East Side, where he'd crash on his new-found friends' couches. Once again, he had to resort to taking up more ridiculous odd jobs to get by. He found himself taking ID photos for the YMCA on the Upper East Side (the job lasted two weeks), being a hot dog waiter at children's parties, and then moving on to checking book sleeves in a bookshop in the East Village. What was important for Beck, though, was that he was hanging out with like-minded people. As he told Thora-zine magazine, 'I just spent a couple of years sleeping on couches, being penniless. Just making music. There's just all these people there making music and there's always a place to crash, and there's always something going on every night.'

Musically, Beck moved on from covering old Woodie Guthrie songs to nurturing the germ that was to eventually become his own unique sound. It was in the East Village that the so-called anti-folk scene was positively thriving. It was like a musical war between punk and '60s folk, resulting in musicians, and anyone else who drifted in off the street, screaming along to folk songs in a no-holds barred anarchic free for all. 'It was a response to this sort of easy listening thing that folk music had come to mean', Beck explained to The Guardian's Dave Bennun. It was here that he happened upon a kindred street musician-cum-erstwhile street poet, who performed a song to him about potato chips. Beck soon found himself drawn to the run-down clubs that celebrated this scene - the Chameleon (a bar on 6th Street) and the ABC No Rio - and started to make regular appearances on their 'open mike' jam nights. As he told Barney Hoskyns of Mojo, 'I had my guitar and there was this whole kinda punk-rock-folk scene and noise-music-chaos-poetry-underground-basement-40-ounce-malt-liquor-being-crazy scene going on.'

Beck couldn't have found a more perfect place to experiment with all the different influences he'd been juggling with. And it spawned his realisation that he could combine whatever styles he wanted to, and sing about whatever entered his head at the time, no matter how crazy or mundane. He'd often join in on other artists' surrealistic over-enthusiastic turns, where experimentation was not only accepted but enthusiastically encouraged, and the more obscure they were, the better. His gigs, however, weren't limited to the scummy anti-folks bars. He also pestered friends to let him support them at their gigs in scummy punk clubs, including opening for early gigs for the then-struggling San Fransiscan punkers, Green Day.

Six

BACK IN L.A.

In 1990, after around two years of slumming it in New York, he was finding it increasingly difficult to find work to support even his frugal lifestyle. He was also missing the warmer climate of the West Coast, so he decided to scrimp the money together to get him back home.

When he returned to LA, he found that very little had changed. It wasn't too long though before things started getting exciting - the growing coffeehouse scene around the Silverlake area had really started kicking off. Described by Billboard at the time as being 'One of the most dramatic buzzes to come out of the Los Angeles music scene in nearly a decade.' With his growing repertoire of songs, he blagged his way into playing in-between other people's sets at the Fuzzyland (the club which changed location for every show), the Onyx, Highland Grounds and the Pik-Me-Up. He took part in the Silverlake Street Festival, and started getting irregular support slots at the soon-to-be-legendary Jabberjaw coffeehouse.

Beck found that most of the already established bands and musi-

cians were frustratingly reticent in offering him support slots. There were, however, a couple of exceptions. As he told UHF, 'Carla Bozulich of the Geraldine Fibbers and Possum Dixon were really receptive, which is really a hard thing to find in LA. Most of the time, there isn't any kind of musical community, there isn't any kind of connection between bands, so when I met those people, it was more of a family.'

His musical style was to bring his pure folk, country and blues influences and back it with the beat of the only contemporary style he saw fit to listen to at that time - hip-hop, the modern blues. 'I knew my folk would come alive if I put hip-hop beats behind it', he told The Face, moving him to reject the notion that he was into out-and-out white boy rapping, preferring to describe his style as 'talking blues.'

It was around this time that Beck started to compile and distribute cassettes of his music. Beck's motivation to get his music heard though wasn't through a desire to be recognised. As he told Blah Blah Blah, 'I wasn't hawking them or anything. It was like someone putting out a 'zine. I was just doing my own thing ...'

In early 1991, Tom Rothrock, Brad Lambert and Rob Schnapf, the owners of LA's Bong Load Custom Records, mosied over to the Jabberjaw club on one of their regular jaunts to check out what was happening. By lucky coincidence, it was one of the infrequent nights when Beck had been able to beg his way onto the bottom of the bill. The three guys were blown away by Beck's short set, immediately recognising his massive potential. This was to be the turning point in Beck's currently anonymous musical career, although it was to take a while before things really started to get moving.

It was through Tom Rothrock, who thought Beck should lay some of his tracks down, that he was first introduced to an underground and respected LA hip-hop producer, Karl Stephenson. Beck's interest was kindled when he was told that Stephenson had not only produced a Ghetto Boys record, but that he also had an eight-track in his house. Up until then, Beck had had no access at all to producing and mixing his songs, everything he'd done had been solo, his cassette recorders and his acoustic guitar, and, although made with the best of intentions, his DIY tapes were positively lo-fi lo-fi.

It wasn't long before he decided to take Rothrock up on his advice, and got together with Stephenson. It was in these early recording sessions in Stephenson's living room that he laid down the first rap track he'd ever written - Loser , which was to consequently launch him into international recognition.

The recording of his first tracks were fragmented affairs. He'd be rushing to finish laying down guitar tracks and vocals, before scurrying off when Stephenson's girlfriend was due to arrive back from work. Loser started off with Beck laying down the slide-guitar, Stephenson then recording it, looping the drums and, as Beck instructed, backing it with his preferred hip-hop beat, and incorporating a sample from Dr Johns I Walk On Guilded Splinters. Four hours later, the track was finished. And, for quite a while, was to be forgotten about.

Seven

LOSER

Loser wasn't to see the light of day for nearly two years. After collecting an inch of dust in Stephenson's apartment for about a year, he dug it out and brought it to the attention of the guys who'd originally hooked Beck up with him, Bong Load Custom Records. They immediately went ahead, and pressed 500 12-inch 45rpm vinyl copies of Loser, backing it with another of the tracks recorded during these early sessions, Steal My Body Home (which was to later appear on Mellow Gold). They circulated them amongst their friends and the influential US college radio stations, who immediately started playing the song to death.

It was soon to become the most requested song to be played by the students, and the stations who hadn't been lucky enough to receive the single in the original mail-out, started hassling Bong Load for copies. It wasn't long before word started to spread like wildfire, as he told Mike Rubin of Spin Magazine. 'These really heavy-duty commercial stations started playing it. They didn't even have any copies. They were making cassette copies off of someone who had a copy of the vinyl.'

It was in the summer of 1993, that Tony Berg, an A&R man at the mighty major Geffen, by chance heard Loser playing on the radio. He immediately contacted Chris Douridas, the producer of the hugely popular Morning Becomes Eclectic show on the commercial station KCRW, who, in turn, contacted Beck through Bong Load, inviting him to play a live set on the show. Beck arrived at the radio station, performed Loser and another track, MTV Makes Me Want To Smoke Crack, before heading straight back to play that night at LA's Cafe Troy, the coffeehouse which his mother Bibbe co-owned with her Mexican artist husband, the artist Sean Carillo.

The session on Morning Becomes Eclectic produced an amazing response. That night, Beck graduated from playing to a handful of uninterested locals, to attracting a crowd who could have easily filled the small coffeeshop many times over. It was also at Cafe Troy that Beck was to support Black Fag, the punk-performance-art band, fronted by the infamous uber-diva, Vaginal Creme Davis, a 6'7" drag queen, whose guitarist was, in fact, Bibbe.

Almost immediately after his performance on KCRW, the most influential radio stations in the States had Loser on their play lists, including KRQQ, the LA station which is given the credit for breaking Loser big-time. 'I got totally freaked out', Beck admitted to Thora-Zine Magazine when quizzed about the reaction to his single. 'They just took the song and ran with it, and I'm like "Yahoo, I'm back here." '

This is not to say that Beck was desperately unhappy about the

success of Loser, and the subsequent attention which was showered upon him. It was more a definite feeling of disorientation and mystification, as he poetically explained to Blah Blah Blah's Lisa Verrico. 'It was like being dragged onto the rollercoaster, when you were just wandering around the fair. There are a lot of dynamics involved in success. It's new so it's fun. But it's also exhausting. I felt like someone had taken me on a surprise vacation and I hadn't had time to pack a toothbrush.'

On the 5th of March 1994, Gloria Estefan was topping the UK charts, and Loser entered the British charts at number 16, one place behind Meatloaf. That week, Beck made his unforgettable Top of the Pops appearance. A week later it had climbed one place to 15, and the following weeks saw it slowly descending down the charts. But that wasn't to be the end of Loser's legacy to Beck by any means.

The manic buzz which surrounded Loser's chinese-whispers-style meteoric rise into the consciousness of the world's public, soon resulted in a ferocious bidding battle between the USA's most powerful record labels, including Geffen, Capitol and Warner Brothers. It was a time which was particularly unsettling for Beck. Not only because after years of struggling and having no one give him a chance, now suddenly everyone wanted a piece of the action, but also because he'd never seriously considered that his music would be any more than a hugely satisfying hobby.

'I'd been working in a video store and nobody ever took me seriously', he told the Los Angeles Times' Richard Cromelin, 'I'd been playing these clubs, Jabberjaw and Al's Bar. Sometimes, the bands would let me get up in between and play a couple of songs. I couldn't even get my own show. So, I thought the whole thing was a joke. I thought it was all gonna end any day.'

Up until now, he'd obviously had full artistic control of his music, because he was just about the only person to have a vested or any other kind of interest in it. If he was to sign a deal, then there was one thing that he wouldn't compromise on, not even an inch, - how and what he released. 'I try not to compromise on anything', he explained simply in The Face.

Most fledgling artists and bands would party nonstop for weeks, flip backwards and turn cartwheels when they signed their first deal. The most they could hope to bargain for was a promise from the record company to commit to two albums. And for a relatively unknown artist to have all the major labels snapping at your heels, fanning blank cheque books in your face all on the strength of one song, is a rare enough occurrence. But to have one of the most powerful men in the world's music industry allegedly call you up, and let you call all the shots, is about as likely as winning the lottery three weeks in a row.

The fact was that Beck, at only 22 years of age and without any real experience of the way things normally work, was on the ball enough to insist that he had his lawyer Bill Berroll negotiate a contract which would give him the option to release 'uncommercial' records on any independent label whenever he wanted. This says it all. 'The way it works in record companies is that you put out a record every two years', Beck told UHF. 'That era of putting out two albums a year, which I think is very healthy musically, is long gone. But I can put out other records on the side on smaller labels.'

> ' I felt like someone had taken me on a surprise vacation and I hadn't had time to pack a toothbrush.'

So, after months of phone calls, Beck signed to Geffen (home to Nirvana and Sonic Youth) on his own terms. Once Beck had managed to secure himself into a contract which still left him with all the creative license he could possibly need, the matter of hard cash played a very poor second. 'I didn't get that much money' he explained to Thora-Zine Magazine, 'I got enough to pay my rent for a year and buy some equipment and stuff. But it wasn't a money deal. If I wanted money, I could've gotten three times as much.'

Soon enough, he was to share Nirvana and the Beastie Boys' powerful management team - John Silva and his team at Gold Mountain, who continue to guide his career. In the meantime, however, Loser was surging up the charts worldwide. And Beck was to be hailed as the champion of the successors of the earlier 'Generation X' - the new and unimproved Slacker Generation, and a bigger misconception couldn't have been made.

Eight

SLACKER

OK, so you could say that Beck brought the inevitable accusations of being the figurehead of a generation of slackers on himself. He did unwittingly call his single Loser, oblivious to the repercussions it would bring, and if Beck is to be believed, he didn't even know what a slacker was. But if there's one thing which is now known about Beck, and the way he approaches lyrics writing, it is that he wouldn't say something as black and white as this, and mean it.

Beck's obscure and often bizarre streams of (un)consciousness have set him apart from everyone else in his generation. He has a rare ability to turn a phrase by almost upending it, and his clever and unusual play on words and rhyme is evident in even his earliest songs. However, Beck strongly asserts that they aren't supposed to be immediately obvious, or mean any one thing to everyone, as he told Interview Magazine. 'Usually the music inspires the lyrics. The lyrics just sort of fall off like a bunch of crumbs from the melody. That's all I want them to be - crumbs. I don't want to work any kind of fabricated message.'

Despite this, from the start there have been many comparisons to the way in which Bob Dylan wrote in his most prolific period. Beck totally denies that Dylan's an influence on him, as he told The Face.

'It seems like you have to have money to be able to, you know, not do anything.'

'People often ask me if I am influenced by Dylan and the 'Stones, and I say, well, I truly am not. I was into the people that influenced those sixties guys: Woodie Guthrie, Blind Lemon Jefferson, Mississippi Fred McDowell, folk and blues.'

However, Alan Ginsberg the '60s beat poet and Hansen, a close family friend, have been moved to hail Beck's lyrics as the most prolific since Bob Dylan's. They go so far as to call him the voice of his generation. Quite an accolade, considering the fact that Bob Dylan continues to this day to be considered as one of the most important artists of the most musically influential decade of popular music so far. This is because of Beck's ability to rattle out socio-political tunes and cleverly phrased thought-provoking lyrics at an alarming pace. And, as Dylan was considered to be the voice of the anti-establishment youth of his decade, Beck was given his title rather earlier. So, back to slackers.

The Slacker generation was characterised as being lazy, hash-smoking, remote-control toting, Dorito munching Beavis & Butthead mimicking, good-for-nothing layabouts - and damned proud of it. It was the scene which not only celebrated itself, it wallowed in it.

There are, of course, doubts that any such scene ever realistically existed outside the minds of the old sanctimonious blaggers who looked down on America's youth. Though if it did exist, then it certainly wasn't inherent in the kind of kids who came from Beck's poor neighbourhood. More probably it was, as Beck has pointed out, 'a middle-class thing'. To be a slacker cost money: Freetos, Cheese-Whiz and pay-per-channel don't come cheap, and as Beck pertinently commented in Interview Magazine, 'It seems like you have to have money to be able to, you know, not do anything.'

While the kids from Beck's neighbourhood were either trying to drag themselves out of their poverty-entrenched lives, or join the plethora of LA gangs, the middle-class kids were playing at being losers for fun, because they knew very well that when they wanted to, they could escape it. The slacker mentality is close to the student 'animal house' mentality - a short excursion into slumsville. Building walls of beer cans, eating junk food and living like a sleaze is damn fine fun because there's always a way out. Not so cool when there's no foreseeable end to the squalor.

So, as he asserted, Beck's lyrics weren't as black and white as everyone read them. 'Soy un perdidor, I'm a Loser Baby, So why don't you kill me' wasn't an anthem of self-deprecation, and it most certainly wasn't an anthem for slackers everywhere. The truth behind the lyrics was far more personal. At one of his sessions while he was joking about with Karl Stephenson, he was recording the vocals for Loser, and launched himself into a Chuck-D style rap. As he explained to Rick Rubin of Spin, 'When they played it back, I was like "I'm the worst rapper!" So, when I did the chorus I was just putting myself down.' And as he explained to Thora-Zine magazine, 'The chorus should have been, "I can't rap worth shit." '

Beck's obscure reference to his crap-rap was to hang like an albatross around his neck for quite some time, yet he argues that it didn't affect him as much as it could have done. 'I play it all the time', he told Blah Blah Blah. 'It's a real cliché for musicians now to go through great torment about it. They struggle with their deep artistic nature because they're only known for this one song. I don't buy into that.'

Perhaps this is simply because he knew that he was worth more than one song. Unlike the Babylon Zoos of the world, who after the initial hype, can't prove their critics who are hailing them as one-hit-wonders, wrong. Most one-hit-wonders are exactly that. Beck just had to prove that he was more than capable of coming back with songs that would well and truly make them eat their words.

It was when he was listening to the radio one day, that he first heard his song being hailed as the 'slacker anthem of all slacker anthems'. His first reaction to the fact that his words were being taken totally out of their original context was that it was a drag. But, as resulted in just about every interview Beck has ever sat through ever since, it has involved him in setting the record straight, explaining and justifying himself, ...over...

'It was definitely a case of wrong place, right time', he told the NME's Johnny Cigarettes. 'People needed a designated candidate, and I was it. I mean, I didn't even know what a slacker was! But I was too naive to fight it. You do photo shoots, and they say, 'Put this shirt on', 'Sit on this sofa', 'Look tired or something', and it's all perpetuated.'

...and over ...

'You'd have to be a total idiot to say: "I'm the slacker generation guy. This is my generation ..." I'd be laughed out of the room in an instant ... I've always tried to get money to eat and pay my rent and shit, and it's always been real hard for me', he asserted to Spin's Mike Rubin.

..again ...

'A slacker doesn't make records like mine' he insisted in Spin. 'A slacker doesn't work hard getting his music right.'

Beck may not have known anything about slackers before Loser, but he was probably to become the most informed person on the 'Generation X' ever. And, not being one to take his responsibilities lightly (he may not have felt any affinity to them, but he was, you remember, inextricably attached to them through proxy), he wasn't without his own unusual solutions.

'I'm going to get this gigantic 40-foot-wide pair of pants and get all the kids to get in the pants with me, and we're going to do aerobics' he joked in Spin. 'The problem with these kids is they've just gotta get in shape. I'm just going to be sort of the exercise instructor. A human aerobics tape, if you will.'

It never happened, sadly. Although his hand-me-down flares admittedly started getting wider. However, Beck was quick to chastise all the kids who turned up to his gigs wearing the Subpop T-shirts, emblazened with the slogan Loser. One night, at LA's Cafe Troy, he asked, 'What's with all these Loser T-shirts? Don't you people have any self-respect', following this by launching into a song called Teenage Wastebasket.

So, although everyone was concentrating on Loser, his first Geffen album was released on its back in March 1994. And it was positively crammed with outlandish, scatterbrained references to 'tofu the size of Texas', belly flops in pools of yellow sweat and there was even a Nightmare Hippy Girl thrown in, but there was certainly no slack clap-trap in sight.

Ten

MELLOW GOLD

The recording and mixing of Mellow Gold was finished in just two weeks on an incredibly frugal budget of $500. He laid down some new tracks, but in the main, opted for using the tracks he'd laid down on the 8-track with Karl Stephenson, including Steal My Body Home (Loser's original B-side). Considering the fact that Beck had been so hard to pin down to sign his record contract, it's surprising that he decided not to use Geffen's money to enlist a big-name producer. Instead, he opted to use people that he knew and trusted, and who he'd been working with for some time: Stephenson, Bong Load's Tom Rothrock and Rob Schnapf, and, of course, himself.

The cover of Mellow Gold is anything but mellow, featuring a sculpture entitled 'Last Man After Nuclear War', created by Beck's friend, Eddie - the long-haired dude who made cameo appearances in both the Loser and the Where It's At videos. The sculpture, made from a nitrous inhaler, screws and various odds and ends, looks like the last mutant cyborg set against a backdrop of fiery bomb-blast clouds.

The impetus for the lyrical content on the album stemmed from Beck's surroundings over the couple of years that the songs were written. As he explained to Interview Magazine. 'All these things came out of the landscape like horrible fumes, something acidic and rancid that you breathe in. Like the smog - you don't have to breathe it, but you can't help it 'cause it's there. You have no choice.' (This feeling comes across strongly in the first verse of Pay No Mind (Snoozer).

More precisely, the surreal lyrics for the tracks on the

album stemmed from Beck's impoverished experiences in LA in the late 80s - his demeaning jobs and the people he was hanging out with. He'd lace the storytelling with the most unlikely dreams and nightmare scenarios and stories, some true and some just plucked from his weird imagination to entertain himself more than anything else, and all littered with references to chickens, wet cigarettes and the devil.

On Soul Suckin Jerk, Beck quits his job, burns his uniform and roams around the streets of LA in only his underwear (something he actually did with his friends as a dare), sharing a fake-fur coat with a hooker, stealing a policeman's gun and going berserk on the rooftops firing the gun into the mall (something we can safely assume that he didn't do outside of his imagination).

'One of my friends I wrote a song about, got drunk at a fair, went on the ferris wheel and threw up over everybody. The other thing comes out of working in a deadend job, where you're this subhuman grunt, your boss doesn't know your name and you're not even getting paid enough to eat', he recalled in the UK broadsheet The Guardian.

Some of the tracks have obvious origins, like Beercan, with more lucid references to his leaf-blowing job. Others are more obscure. The introduction to Truckdrivin' Neighbors Downstairs (Yellow Sweat) could have been taken straight from Andy Warhol's film, Chelsea Girls. Starting with a poorly recorded angry exchange between two drugged-up prima donnas.

Although it was to be Beck's first major label album release, due to the way it was compiled and rushed through - some of the tracks being his earliest - it was something of a hotchpotch. 'Maybe half of it was cohesive', Beck explained to Select, 'and then there were other things just tossed in there that weren't really intended to be released.' Yet he conceded, 'I think it works together.'

Beck has consistently explained in interviews that the making of Mellow Gold was recorded with humour, making up surrealistic ramblings to entertain himself, his friends and Karl Stephenson. It is totally believable that the record was made without knowing that the songs would ever be released because of its lack of continuity. His vocal style varied wildly from camped-up, Mid-West characterisation in Beercan, drunken drawling in Truckdrivin' Neighbors Downstairs, eerie Dalek-manipulations in Steal My Body Home and the atmospheric LSD tripped-out, slowed-down vocals in Mutherfuker.

However, he didn't feel that he hadn't taken the songs on Mellow Gold as far as he would have liked. Because it was such a low-budget affair, recorded exclusively in a cheap 8-track studio, it was to take him some time to start to appreciate his first major label album. 'I was always trying to make it sound as good as I could. I was embarrassed by a lot of my songs because of the way they sounded', he told The Face in 1996. 'This was way before lo-fi became hip. I was ashamed of my music because it was so badly recorded.'

Although Beck had major reservations about Mellow Gold, in hindsight, two years later, he started to see its value. 'OK, so Mellow Gold wasn't as good as it could have been, but it was new, and that's what counted to me', he admitted to The Face. Beck didn't even play the album once it had been released, and it wasn't until the summer of 1995, over a year afterwards, that he could bring himself to listen to it again. 'I couldn't believe I liked it', he exclaimed in Blah Blah Blah. 'I spent months touring, thinking I had to get another record out because Mellow Gold was so embarrassing. Then I heard it and thought it was kind of silly but also fun.'

The music critics didn't subscribe to his initial feelings. It was critically acclaimed as a brilliant debut album, with more than a taster of the potential he would hopefully realise. A review of Mellow Gold by Paul Evans in Rolling Stone typified the general consensus about the album:

'A true up-from-underground anthem, a sly '90s twist on Dylan's Subterranean Homesick Blues, Loser was an awesome,

'This was way before lo-fi became hip. I was ashamed of my music because it was so badly recorded.'

omnipresent single, its trickle-of-consciousness lyrics, ragged acoustic six-string and noise percussion lingering on the radio waves like air freshener. Even more remarkable was the fact that the rest of Mellow Gold kicked just as cleanly. Beercan, Steal My Body Home, Blackhole, Truckdrivin Neighbors Downstairs (Yellow Sweat) - the entire joint smoked with mordant wit and engaging self-assurance.

'Coming more or less out of nowhere, Beck fashioned one of those rare novelty records that remain surprising. The linguistic daring and musical integrity of this fetching poster-boy- for- loser chic, ensure that Beck will be winner in the long run.'

The comparison of Beck to Bob Dylan came thick and fast, despite Beck's protestations otherwise, but considering his folk-influenced strummings, it was inevitable. Straight after Loser on the album came Pay No Mind (Snoozer) - a simple, laid-back acoustic take, interspersed with haunting harmonica, reminiscent of Dylan's The Times They Are A Changing. The lyrics are an inventive play on words, ironic as individual soundbytes, but almost nonsensical as a whole - unless, of course, you are Beck. 'He might be singing about himself, knowing, as he seems to, the ebb and flow of rock's fickley cycle spin. He's a protest singer for the irony age, chronicling the punchline, not the breadline', Spin's Mike Rubin commented.

However he was described, placing him into the rigid musical categories was a little more difficult. Beck is truly one artist who defies simplistic categorisation. Perhaps Time Out hit the nail on the head, by describing it as a 'funk/rock/hip hop/folk/Blues/Latin mèlange.' So, they kept their options well and truly open, but neglected to mention a couple of his major influences - punk and country - which Beck has described as being in there somewhere as well.

What was inevitable, though, was that despite the acclaim that Mellow Gold received, after such a massive hype for such an unknown star, there's always going to be a backlash. And, it wasn't long before the phrase 'one-hit wonder' was to be bandied about whenever Beck was mentioned.

Eleven

BECK

So, Mellow Gold went to the Top 10 Stateside, and although it fared less well in the UK, only making it to number 41, it sold nearly a million copies in the months following its release. Nevertheless, the success of Loser dragged Beck like a cowboy attached to the stirrup of a runaway horse around the world, taking in Europe, Australia, Japan and the US. He toured constantly, was put in front of TV cameras, was interviewed, photographed, scrutinised and hailed as the weirdest little fella around. ('I find all that "Beck the Manchild" insulting', he later commented in The Face).

Had Beck realised that it was to be a couple of years before he was in a position to release another record, Mellow Gold may well have been a different affair altogether, as he told Lisa Verrico of Blah Blah Blah. 'Mellow Gold was just a bunch of songs I'd done over a three year period. I wanted to follow it up immediately with a proper studio album, but the success of Loser foiled that plan.'

So, despite the critical success of Mellow Gold, Beck continued to be portrayed as an unknown slacker who'd recorded the ultimate slacker anthem. He had been jettisoned to the top of the pile of 'Generation X'ers', waving the flag and legitimating the slack way of life, albeit accidentally. Nearly all the songs written for Mellow Gold were, in fact, written in the '80s, way before the slacker thing kicked off. Yet, after the hype and subsequent success of Loser, Beck was to be the subject of the inevitable backlash. 'We were playing a show, and in the newspaper it said, "There are only two words for Beck: "Tommy Tutone" ' Who? Well, quite. But, what was so discouraging for Beck was that Loser was just a small fragment of his massive repertoire - four hours in Karl Stephenson's house. And a flippant off-the-cuff remark about this dismal attempt at rapping, was to have long-term repercussions. Not only did he have to prove himself to be more than the sum of one song, but he also had to fight against the unwarranted label which had been bestowed upon him.

What was equally discouraging, was that some of the people who'd gotten into Beck, on the weight of Loser, were equally disparaging. During the exhausting tour schedule following Mellow Gold, when all that Beck wanted to do was get back to the studio to record

LASH

his second Geffen album, he was faced with crowds who only came to see him so they could hear him perform Loser. He describes one of the Lollapaloza shows, after a particularly blank-faced response from the audience, as 'a neutral experience.' At another show in San Diego, Beck recounts an even more nullifying experience in Blah Blah Blah.

'There were around 300 people there. I played Loser, then looked up at the audience and at least 200 of them had left. I couldn't work out whether some magician had come and vanished them, or if a toxic gas had gone off and disintegrated them. Six months after Loser, that could never happen, because all the kids that weren't really into my music had left me for the next hip thing - 'Weezer' probably.'

Around the time Loser hit the scene, The Offspring were to rise to fame through their release of the US punk anthem Self Esteem, from their second Epitaph album - the multi-million seller Smash. Their lead singer, Dexter Holland, sang 'I know I'm being used, that's OK man 'coz I like the abuse, I know she's playing with me, that's OK coz I've got no self esteem ...I may be dumb but I'm not a dweeb, I'm just a sucker with no self esteem.'

Just as the press surrounding Loser was waining, it was brought back to the forefront of media attention yet again by articles appearing in broadsheet newspapers and magazines, and by academics and social commentators scrutinising, offering theories about and analysing the so-called slacker generation. Yet again, they got it all wrong by reading too much into the often tongue-in-cheek lyrics penned by rock bands. Self Esteem had, in fact, been written by Dexter Holland and his wife, and rather than being a song of self-hatred, it was a collaboration which amused the couple. This, of course, didn't stop the ruminations.

Despite the 'one-hit wonder' tag slapped upon him, Beck was surprisingly unperturbed. His only reaction to his critics was to continue with his hectic workload, while simultaneously working on new tracks for his various projects and his second album for Geffen.

Twelve

WORKAHOLIC

'The image of me as a workaholic hermit is all true. No, not really, but I do spend an inordinate amount of time writing and recording. It's just always been necessary to do that, to get deeper into it', he admitted in the NME. So, from the minute he signed his deal, Beck hasn't stopped. Hardly surprising, then, that between Spring 1994 and Winter 1995, he'd written over 70 songs, and he was releasing material all over the place.

The only other single to be taken from Mellow Gold was to be Beercan, the song which was lyrically based on his dead-end jobs in LA, but it made relatively little impact on the charts, before fizzling out.

At the same time, Beck, true to this original premise of releasing other material on independents, did so at a frantic pace. They all sold respectably, and enjoyed considerable underground success, with all the die-hard fans collecting Beck's never-ending stream of releases. It's All In Your Mind was put out on Olympia WA's K Records, and by the summer of 1994 he also managed to release two albums, both recorded at about the same time, yet wildly different. One Foot in the Grave, which has been cited by Rolling Stone as his 'finest, lyrically and emotionally consistent', was an album he put together with The Beat Happening's Calvin Johnson, and was put out by K. It leaned towards Beck's laid-back, folksy roots, yet Stereopathic Soul Manure released by Flipside, veered on the side of experimentalism with harder and more fragmented noisebytes.

Although Loser was the first single everyone associates with Beck, his first release was MTV Makes Me Want To Smoke Crack, a 7-inch released on Flipside Records in January 1993. In between Bong Load Custom distributing the original 500 copies of Loser and its official release on DGC in January 1994, Bong Load also released another Beck 7-inch sin-

'People talk about apathy among our generation,

gle, Steve Threw Up in December 1993. Also, in January 1993, Sonic Enemy released Golden Feelings, a cassette comprising of 17 early Beck tracks, now deleted. It was already becoming extremely difficult to keep track of Beck's discography.

Around the time MTV picked up on Loser, and played it in heavy rotation, they became aware of the single, MTV Makes Me Want to Smoke Crack, which they immediately used as a backing track to one of their trailers. 'If someone attacks you and you turn it into a T-shirt, then you pretty much render it powerless', he told the NME's Johnny Cigarettes. 'But I wasn't putting down MTV, I was just commenting on what it is. It's an alternative consciousness, which is like being on crack.'

Not that Beck would know about crack - he apparently doesn't take drugs. And when he wrote the song, he hadn't even seen MTV. 'I was blissfully ignorant', he admitted in Spin. Although MTV bore the brunt of his attack of television, he is wary of the whole phenomenon of the whole shebang. Television to Beck, is a modern evil, which distracts and pacifies his peers from doing more interesting and gratifying things. 'We've lost the ability to think about our inner life at all. We're always looking to outside forces to

stimulate us, TV or whatever.' Beck commented to Cliff Jones of The Face.

Beck's opinion of television in general, with it's fragmented and unreal scenarios and society's preoccupation with it, has led him to theorise on its effect on society as a whole, distracting people from being themselves and using their time more constructively. He has gone so far as to say that some of his acquaintances have become caricatures of the already gross caricatures.

'People talk about apathy among our generation, but you know, it's all TV', he told the NME's Johnny Cigarettes. 'Everything's making a joke out of something. And everybody's using funny voices all the time ... It's out of control, embedded in what they are. It means no one develops their own personality, they just pick one off the TV. That's a strange predicament when you don't know who you are.'

So, without the evil of television to distract him from doing more creative things (he has stopped watching it altogether, apart from a few and far between channel surfing sessions in hotel rooms), Beck continued writing and touring like a man possessed. Once Loser and Mellow Gold had been released, touring was to take him all over the world for the next 18 months.

but you know, it's all TV'

Thirteen

TOURING

IN the summer of 1995, Beck joined Elastica, Sonic Youth, Hole, Cypress Hill, Pavement and The Jesus Lizard on the Lollapaloza tour. His support slot on the European leg of Sonic Youth's tour in mid-1996, saw him enthusiastically trying to woo venues packed to the hilt with Sonic Youth's hardcore punkcore posse. And at times this turned out to be a nigh on impossible task, as he told Gina Morris of Select.

'Well, it's interesting. Doing all these old folk songs in front of a rock audience, they tend to get a little agitated and talkative. But I'm used to dealing with this kind of crowd. I used to play between bands at clubs, after I got bored and blew the cafe scene. I used to come up with all kinds of things to get their attention. A lot of my songs became really silly, just to shock people. I had my reservations about doing this, obviously, but it's great.'

Mark Luffman of the Melody Maker, didn't share his opinion. In his review of Beck's support slot to Sonic Youth in Madrid, in their April 13th 1996 issue, he wasn't backward in coming forward with his unfavourable opinion.

'Into all this cultural confusion steps Beck, a man famous for an anthemic nihilistic rap-attack two years ago that he's been trying to live down ever since. The news from Madrid is - he's failed. One song into his pitiful acoustic set and the crowd have had enough. "Ammma lloooozah babbeeee" they shout. Beck ignores them and they give up, chatting effortlessly over the top of the next three songs. "Yeah, I'm real sorry to interrupt here. I'm sure you've got really important things to chat about", Beck sneers.

Unfortunately, the locals' insouciance means bottling is beneath their dignity. Beck doesn't deserve to get away with this. Mediocre songs, sung poorly, played worse. What makes Beck think we give a shit? By the time he finally does a rap song it's too late. The crowd have gone from cool to glacial, treating Beck's request for dancers from the audience with casual contempt. The girls who do reluctantly allow themselves to be dragged up on stage, stop dancing before it's all over, hustling hastily off stage, hoping no one noticed them. Beck tries to blame the audience for his own sheer crapness with some lame sarcasm. We all ignore him.'

Playing with Sonic Youth was amazing for Beck, no matter what the audience response was, and despite the opinions of certain reviewers. After years of listening to Delta Blues, who were one of the first rock bands, along with Jon Spencer's Pussy Galore, that really got him interested in 'noise music' in his mid-teens', Beck's success enabled him to work and play with his long-time heroes, who he'd regularly been to see as a teenager.

In 1994, he got together with Thurston Moore of Sonic Youth, to record a session for the LA radio station, KCRW. Later in the year, he rapped on Flavor, a track on Jon Spencer Blues Explosion's album Orange, and alongside with Mike D of the Beastie Boys, remixed Flavor for the Blues Explosion's Experimental Remixes album. He also appeared as a sushi chef in the accompanying video.

In the Summer of 1996, he played a solo rootsy hip-hop slot at Australia's Summersault Festival, in-between Sonic Youth and the Beastie Boys, with the latter joining him for an ad-lib grande finale. He also made it over to join the bill on Britain's Phoenix Festival, and was invited out to dinner by one of his fans, the legendary Neil Young.

On the 15th of December 1996, at a packed-out gig in London's Brixton Academy, Beck was inexplicably greeted by flying vegetables hurled at him by the over-enthusiastic crowd. To be honest, it would have been far more surprising had it been women's panties. 'What is it with you English people?' he playfully jibed. 'Did you wake-up this morning and think I must go and buy some sprouts 'cos I'm going to see Beck tonight?'

'You can tell a lot about pop stars from the objects their fans throw on stage during concerts', Sam Taylor of the UK broadsheet The Observer wrote in his review of the gig, trying to explain away the Brussels Sprout Incident. 'From this, one could extrapolate that the 26-year-old American is offbeat, unpredictable, even wacky.'

Perfecting his live performance, is equally as important to Beck as any other aspect of making music. What is extremely important to him is to ensure that all his performances are different in some way. He's quick to criticise those bands who go through the motions every night, telling the same stories, playing the same songs and rarely changing their format from gig to gig. He makes an effort to make every show different, as he explained to Rolling Stone, 'An audience needs someone to get up there and be a complete idiot. If a thousand people are gonna go out of their way to buy tickets and be down with you, you gotta represent. You gotta give it back five times.'

Despite this, he acknowledges that his early performances were far from perfect. Notwithstanding his obvious enthusiasm, his inexperience had an effect on the shows. 'I've become a better musician in the last two years', he told Papermag. 'When I first went on tour, I had never played with a band before and I was trying to keep up with them.'

He also cites the fact that the songs on Mellow Gold were not particularly conducive to successful live shows. As he explained in The Face, 'A lot of Mellow Gold was slow, the songs don't have that live energy that I want when I play with a band.' However, as he became more used to sharing the stage with his band, his confidence grew, and he learnt about the

'... It's always about connecting with the audience, making them laugh or bewitching them, and not doing it too manipulatively.'

dynamics behind entertaining the audience.

Beck started to perfect his on-stage persona, becoming more charismatic and mesmerising. As in his early days in the coffee houses, where he'd make up more and more outrageous lyrics to get the attention of the nonplussed bystanders, Beck used other equally attention-grabbing tricks to keep the fans' attention.

'All the crowd-pleasing devices and tricks can be too simple, so we try to pervert them or do something new with them', he explained to Mojo's Barney Hoskyns. '... It's always about connecting with the audience, making them laugh or bewitching them, and not doing it too manipulatively.'

From his early performances, where he'd slope about self-consciously bouncing and launching into his unique version of break-dancing, with the experience of a year and a half of steady touring under his belt, he started to become more flamboyant. He was no longer a long-haired kid in hand-me down vintage clothes.

By the end of 1996, he'd graduated into wearing dazzling white tassled rhinestone cowboy costumes and tailored suits, had cut his hair and had grown some real whiskers. He was also playing at bigger venues, as his shows started to sell out within days. But if Beck is to be believed, those who managed to get back-stage to meet their hero were pretty disappointed. 'When I play, I'll hang out after my shows and talk to people', he told Papermag, 'but they usually walk away after about five minutes because they find out I'm pretty ordinary.'

Changing his fashion style wasn't the only difference in Beck's live act. By the end of 1996, he had taken to leaping around like an over-enthusiastic punk, lunging into martial arts poses and, of course, continued with his break-dancing. 'I don't do it in a lounge or retro way - that would be too easy' he said, defending his outlandish stage-shows in The Face. 'I try to make it confrontational, taking a cliché and ripping it apart with snot flying out of its nose and asphyxiation.'

Another aspect that changes, is Beck's 'band'. If his discography was already reading like Central London's telephone book, his musical family-tree was more like an overgrown forest. 'I know some people think of 'Beck' as a band or just me, but it's more a loose collection of people', he told Select's Gina Morris. 'Since I started, a lot of people have come and gone, mostly friends. I just kidnap them out of other bands and later they escape back to them ...It has worked to a greater or lesser degree in the past. Sometimes really well, sometimes a complete disaster, but it keeps it interesting.'

After Lollapaloza, his bass player was recruited by Elastica to replace Annie Holland. One of his guitarists joined the Lollapaloza organiser Perry Farrell's Porno for Pyros, and the guitarist previous to him, Chris Ballew, who he'd also collaborated with on the Casper and Mollusk 7-inch, was swiped away by the Presidents of the United States of America. His amazing backing band of elderly gents on Top of the Pops lasted for one appearance only (the truth of the matter was that they couldn't play), and the guy behind the mixing desks who joined him on his tour in late '96 and '97, Theo, once played with Ravi Shankar. In between the hectic tour schedule, releasing albums on independents and appearing on countless compilation LPs, he was fervently writing tracks for his second Geffen album, which he was hell-bent on releasing as soon as possible.

Fourteen

THE MAKING

'**I** was so exhausted after touring with Mellow Gold and the whole overload of the Loser thing that I probably should have taken six months off', Beck admitted to Mojo's Barney Hoskyns. 'But I had all this stuff I needed to get out and I wanted to push myself. I was afraid that otherwise I might settle like a stone at the bottom of the ocean and just stay submerged forever.'

Beck's initial aspirations for his second Geffen album was to produce one dedicated entirely to hip-hop. But over the 18 months he was was working on it, his agenda started to change, as he found that a good proportion of the 40 tracks he eventually laid down were melody orientated. However, he was determined that it would be an album more rhythmic than Mellow Gold and one which would get people dancing.

After taking just two weeks to get Mellow Gold together, Beck wanted to spend as much time as possible to tweak his second Geffen offering into a shape he'd be satisfied with. It was the first record he'd made which he knew was going to be released, and with the massive stockpile of songs he'd been working on for the two years since Mellow Gold, he had an excess of material he wanted to both lay down and play with. So the whole of 1995 was spent fervently recording and mixing, when he wasn't travelling the world on tour. Once again, Beck found that he had little time and no inclination to slack.

His choice of producers stemmed from what was initially to

have have been a short collaboration. Beck hooked up with the Dust Brothers, a.k.a. John King and Mike Simpson, late in 1994, because he didn't have anywhere stable were he could set up a studio. Aware that the Dust Brothers had everything set up in LA's Silverlake Hills area, which was convenient for him as they lived just two blocks away from his home, he got together with them to record a one-off song. Three months and 12 tracks later, the album was already shaping up, and his collaboration with the Dust Brothers was to produce the bulk of the album.

The Dust Brothers had most famously produced the Beastie Boy's 1989 album Paul's Boutique. This album, which despite being a slow-grower and originally pretty much ignored, has since been credited as being a groundbreaking record in hip-hop, setting new and exciting standards in sampling. Once they got to work, the threesome spent a lot of time purging their diverse and eclectic record collections, brainstorming, experimenting and sampling, until the original chords Beck had in mind for the songs were eclipsed and improved upon.

Despite the fact that Beck isn't musically trained, learning to play new instruments comes relatively easily to him. This is evident from the fact that Beck played most of the instruments on the album, including guitar, sitar, bass, keyboards, wind instruments, harmonica and percussion. Beck's rare ability to pick up any instrument and master it within a few hours amazed John King, who recalled a memorable incident in Dazed & Confused. 'He (Beck) looked in the Recycler one day,

OF ODELAY

and saw that a guy in Santa Monica was selling Indian instruments. Two hours later he came back with a sitar and tamboura. He said, "The guy tuned it up for me and taught me how. Let's record something" '

While many of the samples on album were laid down in the Dust Brothers' PCP Labs, taken from Beck's noodlings, they also sampled noise and melody bytes from works as diverse as Schubert's Unfinished Symphony, James Brown's Out Of Sight and Bob Dylan's It's All Over Now Baby Blue. Beck also enrolled the services of various other musicians including the professional skater/musician Paulo Diaz, the Beastie Boys' long-time keyboard player 'Money' Mark Nishita and Jon Spencer. The instruments which were worked into many of the songs ranged from the obvious, to tablas, the saranghi, clarinet, and piano.

Beck was also to work with other producers on three of the album's tracks. Ramshackle was produced and mixed by Bong Load Custom's Rob Schnapf and Tom Rothrock, who also worked together with Beck on Mellow Gold. For Minus, he got together with Mario Caldato Jr. (who also worked on the Beastie Boys' Paul's Boutique) and Brian Paulson, and for the final track on the album Diskobox he got an eager Jon Spencer to work with the Dust Brothers and himself.

Although the album was to take nigh on 18 months from start to being released, not all of the tracks were to be worked and reworked. The New Pollution, which was to be the third single off the album, took only four hours to record, although Beck has since admitted to originally hating it.

During the recording of the album, Beck's grandfather, Al Hansen, died aged 68 (Beck performed several songs at his memorial service). He also saw he passing of various other close friends including Jac Zinder the LA club promoter/music writer (who ran the Pik-Me-Up club where Beck had performed before Loser took off, and who also wrote the first piece on Beck), Leo, his pedal steel guitar player died of cancer, and some of his friends died of Aids.

Beck's reaction to this was not to produce songs which were introspective and sad. As he told Eric Weisband, 'I think more than anything it made me want to make music that was more celebratory.' Straight after coming off the Lollapaloza tour, he went into the studio again with the Dust Brothers and recorded two of the more upbeat and melodic songs off the album, Devil's Haircut and Sissyneck.

Once he was satisfied they had enough tracks that he was happy with, they headed to the more salubrious surroundings of the Conway Studios in the heart of Hollywood, to do the mixing. 'Mixing it was where the real work was', he told Mojo's Barney Hoskyn's. 'Recording it was mayhem, but mixing it we'd just sit there for hours and hours 'til we turned green.'

Although the album was pretty much finished by the Autumn of 1995, the release date was put forward to mid-1996. He also had to make the decision about which of the 40 tracks they'd laid down to put on the tracklist.

Fifteen

ODELAY

Beck called the album Odelay, although in various interviews he invented false names including Le Tough (actually the brand of sunglasses he was wearing), Robot Jazz, The Sensuous Casio, The Sexuality of Lynne and Mellow Tinfoil. (Trying to confuse journalists by stretching the truth and making up insignificant facts is something Beck often does to entertain himself). Odelay came from one of the sound engineers writing the title down incorrectly and it stuck. However it derives from 'orale' - Chicano slang which is used to convey a greeting or a feeling of exaltation. 'I was trying to get a sense of the celebratory aspect I've heard in Mexican music', he explained in The Guardian.

The album kicked off with Devil's Haircut, a laid-back funked-up track backed with a repeated four keyboard notes and up-beat drum loop, and was yet again littered with Beck's trademark weird lyrics saluting the devil. When quizzed by Dazed & Confused's Peter Relic about his continued Beelzebub obsession, he said, 'Evil isn't the only dimension to the Devil. He's a comedian, a swinger, a maker of beats. I incorporate him in the way that someone might use Stagger Lee (a Delta Bluesman who, legend has it, murdered a man to fulfil his pact with the devil) as a bad-ass figure, a shadowy presence.

With Mellow Gold, Beck had created stories by working around his experiences living on the breadline in LA, but his change in lifestyle since then had obviously changed his focus.

'... It doesn't really apply to the way life is now, so I'm writing these songs in a vacuum', he told The Guardian's Dave Bennun. 'I have embraced the larger scheme of things and the life that applies to me now. I guess they're just flakier and less substantial times, and that's reflected in the music.'

However, ask Beck what his lyrics are specifically about, and he'll tell everyone a different story - all mythical without a doubt. When asked by Interview Magazine about the lyrics to Sissyneck, he deadpanned , 'Oh, it's the morning after a full night of line dancing and cocaine. It's the achey-breaky heart after the triple bypass. It's a get-together at the recreation centre Ping Pong tournament.'

They should have known better than to have asked. It makes you wonder if he really knows himself. '... Each song creates its own logic', he airily explained to the NME's Johnny Cigarettes who was just as much in the dark about what the hell Beck is actually saying. 'Each song has its own street, its own bathroom and its own ... post office.' Which, of course, doesn't help in the slightest.

Sixteen

WHAT THE CRITICS SAID & THE AWARDS

Considering the fact that Beck hadn't actually released anything on Geffen for nigh on two years, the advance interest in the album was phenomenal. What was so unusual about the situation, was that despite the absence of a follow-up Geffen album, and indeed, his failure to keep the singles coming out to keep everyone's appetite whetted, his reputation as a bit of a musical maverick was continually being built up through word of mouth, and through other musicians voicing their love of his music. Consequently, the expectations for the album were extremely high. Nobody was prepared to accept anything much short of prolific.

Released on the 17th of June 1996, the coverstar was a hurdle-jumping Tibetan sheep dog. This was taken from The Complete Dog Book put out by the American Kennel Club, and some of the collage images on the inslip were done by Beck's late grandfather, Al.

Whatever possessed Beck to select a photograph of a dog for the cover which, incidentally, looked like a supermop is unknown. But what soon became apparent was that Odelay couldn't fail to impress pretty much everyone. It may have confused a few, but it disappointed no one. The album got the US glossies jumping for joy - the way forward to the next millenium was being led by an American. Sighs of relief all round.

True enough, Oasis were taking the world by storm, and their infective melody-driven songs were nothing short of anthemic. But in all honesty, there was little evidence that they were going out of their way to push any of the boundaries of guitar music which had been set by their heroes some thirty years previously. While the Britpoppers were revelling on the ground in all their retro (morning) glory, Beck was working on a higher plane altogether.

Rolling Stone's Mark Kemp was moved to posit, 'Could the future of rock'n'roll be a snot-nosed slacker with a bad haircut, an absurdly eclectic record collection, two turntables and a microphone?', going on to write, 'Odelay takes Beck's kitchen-sink approach to new extremes, while also managing to remain a seamless whole; the songs flow together with intelligence and grace.' The final verdict: 5 out of 5.

Spin joined in on the ebullient praise, 'Beck uses sound and imagery to turn his congested yelp into the voice of a prophet, summoning apocalyptic dread with the chorus "Got a devil's haircut in my mind." I mean who else could bust a rhyme like "Don't be confused when your fuse is up/ And you're taking a leak into your brother's cup" ,and make it sound deep, like a jeremiad for hard times?' Chris Norris also queried : 'Even if it offers no youth-cult manifesto, the warm and inclusive spirit running through this endlessly fascinating album makes Beck something just shy of heroic, whether he wants to be or not.' Scores on the doors: 10 out of 10.

'Possibly the hippest person in the world'

What the songs actually

The UK monthly, Select, couldn't do much but agree. 'Despite the chaos, Odelay isn't likely to scare anyone. The prevailing mood is a dayglo, good-time one. Beck seems to be less interested in being the New Pop Messiah than in being a Lovin' Spoonful for the '90s ... What this amiable nonsense has to say about the State of American Youth is probably nothing at all. What it offers in terms of sprawling entertaining is plentiful indeed.' Marks out of 5: 4.

The rest of the UK music monthlies were just as impressed with Odelay, with Andy Gill of Mojo describing it as 'Intriguingly eclectic and occasionally bordering on the sensible.' While Q's Stuart Maconie gave it 4 stars, and wrote, 'Possibly the hippest person in the world ... Beck might be what that misunderstood visionary Owen Paul meant by his "favourite waste of time"' . Blah Blah Blah's editor, Shaun Phillips, handed himself the task of reviewing the album, pertinently commenting, 'What the songs actually mean are anybody's guess ... but almost everything here rewards those who are willing to give the record a closer inspection. Odelay lives up to Blah Blah Blah's rule of thumb: if it isn't hard work, it isn't any good.'

The only person to voice reservations was to be NME's editor, Steve Sutherland. In his review for the NME monthly Vox, he commented, 'Where Dylan or Syd Barrett or even Steven Jones of Baby Bird would have us fretting over some enigmatic couplet that implies the awful truth, that maybe heaven and hell are, indeed, the same place, Beck just wibbles on about having a devil's haircut in his mind. It's comic book stuff and it just won't wash. There are too many real mad folks out there to escape by playing the fool', awarding it a mediocre 6 out of 10.

However, somewhat unsurprisingly, the UK daily broadsheets followed in line with the general consensus and joined the crowd, adding their cry of 'oralè' to the fanfare for Odelay. The Observer concluded , 'He mixes soft pop country with grunge guitars, heavy hip-hop and '60s jazz kitsch. If that sounds like a mish-mash, the album is just that, but an addictive sweet-sour mash. Interestingly, while others swoon over Lennon and McCartney, Beck has more of the spirit of George and, er, Ringo. He's now sorted himself out with "a stolen wife and a rhinestone life"'.

The Guardian's Jonathan Romney pertinently noted that, 'The 14 tracks here aren't songs so much as essays in delerium, obsessively layered rambles that refused to take the path of least resistance', although he wasn't entirely without his minor reservations, 'Sometimes the bargain basement clutter is just too much to absorb, but at its best, Odelay is a supremely frazzled pleasure.'

Whatever the opinions, Odelay slid into the US charts at number 16 and at number 18 in the UK charts (the third highest new entry behind Louise's debut album, and, ahem, The Smurfs Hits '97 - Volume 1).

Beck started touring again to promote the album, released Where It's At and Devil's Haircut, both taken from the album, and both achieving respectable chart positions, before the end of 1996. 1996 also saw Johnny Cash (who Beck once supported) cover one of his songs, Rowboat, and Noel Gallagher, the Aphex Twin and Mo-Wax artist U.N.K.L.E were all scrambling to re-mix the single Devil's Haircut (the Aphex Twin re-mix entitled Richard's Hairpiece appearing on the B-side of The New Pollution).

The end of year polls prominently featured Beck and Odelay, including Rolling Stone not only giving Odelay the accolade of 'Album of the Year', 'for his unaffected exuberance, fervent eclecticism, precocious ingenuity and stubborn refusal to take himself seriously, Beck Hansen is rock'n'roll's Man of the Year - even if he looks as if he's only 12 years old' they wrote. He was also to have the title of Critics 'Artist of the Year' bestowed upon him, hailing him as 'the arbiter of rock'n'roll's future.' His videos for Where It's At and Devil's Haircut were also in the running for Best Video, but just missed out. Spin voted him 'Performer of the Year', and he was voted 'Best Solo Artist' by the readers of the NME to get his first NME Brat Award.

In 1997, the nominations in the polls continued. Odelay beat it's nearest rivals, The Fugees album The Score, Tricky's Pre-Millenium Tension and Pulp's Different Class, by scoring twice as many points as it's nearest rival (The Fugees) to run away the Village Voice's 'Best of Album of 1996' poll. The Brits hailed him 'Best International Male Solo Artist', and he was also nominated for three (count 'em) Grammies.

Although he missed out on Best Album at the award event held on the 26th of March, he managed to scoop the other two - 'Best Alternative Performance' for Odelay and 'Best Male Rock Vocal Performance' for Where It's At. On being nominated, he commented in Entertainment Weekly, 'It was a little surreal to be nominated. But it feels good to be validated, to be acknowledged. Somehow the perception has changed, and I'm grateful.' Straight after the Grammies and Brit Awards, interest in Odelay was given a positive boost, and saw the album jumping 10 places from 29 to 19 (still failing to overtake The Smurfs, who were still riding high four places above him!).

And whereas previously, his live shows had attracted a mixed and confused response, even the usually cynical UK weeklies united in their praise for Beck, further legitimating his increasingly outlandish shows. The week after returning to the UK , he performed two shows in London and Cardiff which sold like hot cakes and had the touts scurrying around outside charging extortionate prices for a golden ticket.

Amongst those who watched on were: Helena Christensen, Christian Slater, Michael Stipe, Noel and Liam Gallagher ... and Simon Price of Melody Maker who could hardly contain his enthusiasm for the London show at Kilburn National Ballroom, writing, '... this man is da punk with the daft funk, a screeching preacherman prancing about in a pimp's wardrobe and dallying around on a sprawling, drawling, y'all-ing country tip.

'With a lot of old-skool scratching. See, the fundamental beauty about tonight is that the wobblingly vast majority of BECK!'s audience - safe as Auntie's scrummy apple pies to a punter, apart from when they're engaged here by the most inept bar-staffing known to mankind - would sprint barefoot a thrillion miles over broken glass to avoid many of the base elements of this show, notably the crashing hip-hop beats, the slip-sliding western guitars and most definitely the noisy little fella shrieking away in the middle of the stage and yelling at them "Y'all look too sexy for your outfit!!!"'

Michael Bonner of the NME wasn't far behind with his overload of gushing hyperbole, in a brilliant attempt at describing Beck's larger than life stage presence. 'Beck leaps on stage, clad in black suit and white tie, looking for all the world like Jimmy Swaggart's errant nephew. Sorry. Did I say leap? Ah no. He rockets through the air - vroom - like a cat with a box of fireworks up its arse. He bounces, he bodypops, he does crazy legs and throws ridiculously inappropriate Travolta-style poses in a blur of limbs and shiny cufflinks. For the whole evening, too, non-stop. Give the boy some valium before his heart explodes ... But Beck is about more than just putting on a highly entertaining, if mildly deranged, evening. He seems to be making a case for American music, each song reflecting a different genre - from blues to folk to hip hop to grunge - in a unique celebration of its positive qualities.

TO THE

Sixteen

NEXT MILLENIUM

SO, just who the hell is Beck Hansen? And what the hell is he going on about? Ask him, and he avoids giving you a straight answer like an over-suspicious spin-doctor with some half-baked, flaky response. 'An industrial outdoorsman in the petro-chemical-compound-complex loading dock', he enigmatically responded in Vox.

Push him on the matter, and he might give you a half-straight answer: 'Peoples one-dimensional idea of what you are, that sort of slacker idea, or the goofy hip- hop guy, I just think it's silly, it's not me. It's like a cartoon. I'm never going to come up with a synopsi, a "That's it",' he told The Guardian's Dave Bennun in his ever-helpful style.

And whatever it is that's going on his mind, it's being turfed out at supersonic speed. No wonder he needed an open-ended record contract. With 32 songs still on ice from his sessions with the Dust Brothers, make no mistake that Beck intends to release the lot on some disturbingly cool underground label sometime in the future. And, considering the fact that he's continued with his cure-all song-writing production line since he put Odelay to rest in the Autumn of 1995, he's got to have enough songs to keep everybody going into the millenium. Which, if he's to be believed, is when he'll start becoming the prolific artist he's already being hailed as. 'I don't expect to say anything really interesting until I'm at least 50', he stated resolutely to the NME's Johnny Cigarettes. If that's the case, then roll on 2021 ...